Socrates Level Marketing™

"Socrates has a passion for this industry. He has dedicated himself to creating systems for someone simply trying to pay for their product or someone ready to turn it up a notch. This is an entertaining look into the life of a man who failed many times, only to succeed because he had no other choice."

—Kenneth Peavie, Virginia Professional Network Marketer, Certified Physical Trainer, Retired Sargent Major USMC

Socrates Level Marketing™:

Ignite Passion.
Accelerate Your Journey NOW.
Annihilate Limiting Beliefs.

by Socrates Zayas, PhD

ISBN-13: 978-1516866304

ISBN-10: 1516866304

Table of Contents

Foreword:

When I first met Socrates Zayas I knew right away he was a sharp guy. He has an amazing background, he's well educated, he served the United States as a Marine, and he's a family man.

As someone who got his start in the Network Marketing profession as a young man back in 1994, it's wonderful for me to see someone of his stature write a book like this. This book truly dispels the myths surrounding the Network Marketing and Multi-Level Marketing industry and lays out incredible success principals.

This book will serve as blueprint to success for you if you follow it closely. First, it will help you to create the right mindset for success. So few take the time to get their mind right and are in too much of a rush to "just make some money." Second, it will help you develop a real game plan for your Network Marketing enterprise. It will show you how to treat your business like a real business, not a hobby.

Read Socrates Level Marketing™ closely. Implement what you learn. Take massive action. The author has done a phenomenal job here. There is no doubt this book can take years off your learning curve and get you on the fast track to more money and more time freedom.   —Andrew J. Cass, www.AndrewJCass.com

Introduction: Is This Book for Me?

Who is This Book For? Well, it's For YOU!

I'm smiling right now—seriously, it is.

Anyone who hates his or her j-o-b is a candidate for this book. Welcome to Socrates Level Marketing™ principles of multi-level marketing. How will you get out of that job unless you create additional income? If you are too low on money to invest in a business, multi-level marketing is your BEST option. You don't have to stay stuck like a tree in the ground in a situation you don't want to be in. But—and there is always a BUT—YOU must first realize that this is a personal development strategy with profits attached to it. The more you learn, the more you make—which leads me to why it's great for the "I hate my JOB" crowd. You can begin and supplement your lifestyle right now! For some people that is perfectly PERFECT! Three or four hundred dollars a month can make a major difference in the lives of many American families today.

This book is for <u>all sales people</u>.

Yes, you read me right, all sales people. Why? For a few reasons:

1. If you are in sales, you have an unadulterated skill of not fearing the introduction. You have some knowledge of the wheel of the "Sales Cycle" as created by Dale Carnegie, and a "NO" doesn't faze sales people. There are more people you talk to that say no than say yes. Would it be OK to shift your mindset? Could you offer all those people you couldn't sell something to a new way to look at something that you could not only make money with, but also keep making money with? Would it help to even show them how to make money or get their new product for free?

2. Every salesperson has his/her cycle when you're hot and when you're NOT! When you are in a slump, times get hard quickly. Lack of diversification isn't a problem for investors only; it's also a problem for the sales person as well. Realtors might resonate with this one. Many of you make your monies through traditional real estate sales, but then some of you also are, or have been, in the renting and flipping business. You realize that having a stream of consistent income is GOOD! That stream comes with overhead, not to mention the headaches of construction and remodeling, and the market influences your earnings at the time. If you were part of the 2008/2009 crash your profitable real estate became a non sequitur for many. A close friend of mine shared when she had her AH-HA moment. It was when her monthly commission profit from her MLM exceeded her rental real estate profit. AND SHE HAD NO HEADACHE attached. Be careful where all your eggs are. Tough times happen.

3. How old are you? I know—not a politically correct question. But it does effect how sales people perform. MOST sales people get paid per transaction. One transaction—ONE PAYMENT. Zero to hero in 30 days. When day one comes next month, you're back to zero and the grind starts all over again. However, there is a concept called residual income. This is where you sell something one time and continue to get paid on it time after time. Would it be OK, if you learned how to create a stream of consistent and growing profit each and every month

regardless of your age? Some people ask me what I made my first month in network marketing. My response is simple. "Hmmm, I don't know, see I am STILL making money from people I recruited my first month (over 5 years ago). My guess would be that first month has made me hundreds of thousands of dollars. Of course that didn't show up that first month, but it keeps showing up years later." Jump in a time machine, 20 years forward to the future, and walk out to your mailbox. Is there a check there for that sale you made 20 years earlier? NO? Maybe it is time to re-evaluate who is making the fortune off of your life energy, your time.

4. Sales people are the HULK of marketing results. They "SMASH" close.

All Small Business Owners

Forbes.com shared an article, "Would You Join A Multi-Level Marketing Company For Retirement Income?" In it Daria M. Brezinski, Ph.D., a practicing psychologist, is quoted when she interviewed people in MLM. Some said, 'I'm doing this because I'm meeting amazing people…making so many connections" and this is the very reason small business owners should diversify with MLM. It helps to gain more acquaintances and create more community support, which ultimately results in more customers for the small business.

Who Shouldn't Do Network Marketing?

(Maybe I'm crazy but you may NEVER get past this part of the book! FINE, because it's not for everyone, only the sexy people! BOOM!)

If you are any of the following, this marketing strategy, this business model, this vehicle for entrepreneurial freedom isn't for you. In fact you may NOT be entrepreneur material at all.

1. **People that are wussies.** If you are easily affected by other people's opinions, just stick with whatever you are doing. If you are unable to break this addiction to self-image, just stick with whatever you are doing. I had to put my PhD, my Masters of Information Technology, my Biochemistry and my "I'm-this-amazing-intelligent-walking-diploma," behind me. I had to embrace the business and the system. If you care more about the mediocre, and their opinions of you, close this book NOW.

"Do you know what lies at the bottom of the mainstream? Mediocrity."— Death in Venice

---

2. **People with unrealistic expectations.** Your mindset has to do with everything. If you made 100 thousand a year in your JOB, it's because your mindset was like that of a person making $100,000 a year. Realistically, if you didn't make $10,000 a month easily in your last JOB, chances are you won't here either. The good news is this is a personal development system with profits attached. If you do what needs to be done, it will happen.

Invest inordinate amounts of time and effort into self-improvement.

3. **People with negative attitudes.** You suck…sorry, but it's true.

"People want to be around positive people, negative people, unless rehabilitated, don't have a shot at network marketing success." —Ray Higdon

---

4. People who know it all. This is the biggest sickness in ALL industries on the planet and it starts as a child. It drives me crazy when my 7-year-old daughter does something, and I correct her lovingly, and she replies, "I know that!" Really? Because this fishhook I'm digging out of your finger doesn't show me that you actually did know how to set the shrimp on the hook. But, seriously I get it. You have had success in some way, shape or form. I thought I knew it all too, having not one but three separate degrees in totally different industries. I have a Podcast (that's an internet radio show) SocTalks (www.SocTalks.com and on every medium out there). I've been a male physique competitor. As a martial arts practitioner I've earned multiple Black Belts, etc. To quote Tim McGraw, *Can't Tell me Nothin'*. I thought I knew it all, BUT I really didn't. I needed to learn the hard way, and people who excel in this industry must be willing to be coachable and get advice from others.

"If you're drowning how are you possibly going to save someone else? Together you will BOTH drown. Get and learn from a successful mentor, one with a track record of what you want to achieve."—Robert Hollis

---

Chapter 1: What is Socrates Level Marketing™?

Socrates Level Marketing™ is the culmination of information acquired over years attempting to be an entrepreneur. The information in this book I hope will guide you through understanding that wanting something, dreaming about it, and going for it—is just not enough. Especially, not blindly. I hope to explain and deliver actionable steps for you to take your dreams and turn them into reality. How can I know for sure this works? Because I have done it in every possible wrong way, and the minute I humbled myself and submitted to the philosophies, the core principles of multi-level marketing, which I'm going to affectionately refer to as Socrates Level Marketing™, my growth became consistent and continuously upward trending. Why would I call this Socrates Level Marketing™? Because I'm the one who had to learn the hard way, so you don't have to! Once the philosophy was learned, the execution was just elementary and all I needed to do was not to give up.

Why is it You Want to be an Entrepreneur?

For me it was easy. I like nice things. I'm not ashamed to say it, and I am even more in "like" with the idea of providing nice things to those I love. I'm a giver and I'm happiest when giving. My parents, my children, my wife, my closest friends and I have always wanted to give liberally to my college, charities, and yes, even that guy on the street. My problem was that I always ran out of money before I ran out of month! I was always struggling it seemed, and as I write this it strikes me how much more struggle there was than needed be. I tried budgets, technology (apps, and accounting software), jars (literally I saved my cash in jars), all kinds of ideas to make my month shorter and my money longer. My only option was to work harder and longer, so I did to the point I was working eighty percent of the month and the remaining 20 percent I was miserable thinking about the eighty percent, and wondering how I could escape this turbulent insanity. I was caught up in always looking for that better JOB that would pay me more for the exact same thing I was doing. I didn't hop around—don't get me wrong—but I was always looking at the grass on the other side. Ultimately, I changed careers three times.

My Story as an Employee

In my first life I thought the Marine Corps was my ticket. It was actually an institution of do as I say, not as I do. Although I enjoyed the USMC Eagle, Globe and Anchor, it left me yearning for more out of what I thought I was born for. I did learn that I am very tolerable and prefer to work in a TEAM environment with defined goals and missions. This is likely why I fell in love with multi-level marketing and therefore Socrates Level Marketing™.

My second life I spent as a scientist. I became a biology and chemistry major and went to work on infectious disease and genetic research. Wow—right? Sounds so cool. It actually was. It was the advent of HIV, and I totally wanted to be a part of the cure. I was lucky to have had some amazing mentors who never gave up on me and because of this I succeeded in earning my PhD. Thank you Dr. Harold Yaffa and Dr. Guy Bradley. This was the nineties. Science was making huge leaps and bounds monthly. By the end of that decade the mad scientist in his lab was replaced with machines that instead of scientists isolating twenty five hundred genetic base pairs weekly machines were isolating two hundred and fifty thousand base pairs weekly. The only thing increasing abundantly in my life were my bills and this not-so-new hundred thousand dollar student loan. In my mind, my only other alternative was to find a second JOB!

So I did—as an apprentice at a local radio station. My first task there was calling people on the phone and asking them to listen to short snips of country music and rate them—first, if they heard of it before, and second, if they liked or disliked it. Shortly after that I was working in the booth, midnight to 6 AM, five days a week on the radio—but just as the guy who would time the commercials as a national syndicated radio personality did his show. I was so good at it that from time to time I was offered to actually be live on this popular radio station as Steve Kicks, my made up radio personality name. Socrates may have not resonated well with my country listeners and patron-ship. Then back to my day JOB for eight to ten hours, five days a week. I slept where I could and when I could.

My third life as an employee started when one day I heard a commercial. It was for an accelerated master's program in information technology. I jumped all over it. Why was this cool to me? Because I was a closet nerd, a geek that dabbled in hacking and creating programs for my mother's medical business and my friends. I mean really, what was another thing in my life at this point? Long story short, I graduated with honors. Yet, I was so intimidated. I share this not to be judged by you, but to express the fear I was feeling—the doubts and insecurities—about making yet another full career change including an additional fifty thousand dollar student loan. Fear made me set up not one—but five—JOBS, after graduation. I ask you to remember, stop judging. I was nervous, OK? I gave verbal agreement that I would start all five! Yes, I did that! I staggered their start dates by ten days in case one didn't work out, or I just didn't have the skills and got fired, I would still have another one to go to. As luck would have it the first one didn't work out. It was a shady website creation startup and they had no idea what was going on. They actually were less informed than I was and I was out of school like 20 hours. I worked there one day and never returned. I called the next JOB on the list and said, "Hey, I got back earlier than expected." They had me start right away. That was my first validation that this career change was in fact a very good choice. The company was American Express. I was hired there for three times what I made as a scientist and the radio station combined. Everything was good. I had never seen five digits on my pay stub! I started to work at the local colleges and universities part-time, because I felt idle with my time. In some way, I thought that I was giving back. Within six to eight months a very big, yet small, software giant in Palo Alto, California approached me. They needed a special set of skills—someone with an information technology degree and proven teaching skills. They found me through word of mouth and I still, to this day, don't know how I was referred. I suspect it may have been the Director of American Express Business Intelligence, i.e., my boss. He may have felt threatened by my ability and energy. I was known to always be a few steps ahead of everything, and I don't think he knew how to manage my skills. The suitor company flew me to California all red carpet and limo. They interviewed me and slid a paper over to me. It read a whole lot of zeros more than before and a piece of the company too! I started that position in 2000 and stayed with them until 2010 when they released me. Yes, you heard me right! That's a nice way of saying I was fired, with no explanation, no argument, no pat on the back, and no remorse.

What did I learn from this? I learned that there was no loyalty, no TEAM, or sense of duty to someone that lived more in a hotel room and on a plane than with his family. I fought with and charmed so many organizations I can't begin to mention, I'd need a book just for that. This JOB cost me something that is invaluable and could never be exchanged for any amount of money. TIME. I lost time with my son and his two stepbrothers, boys I've loved since they were infants and toddlers. I wasn't there for them really EVER; not from the time I was in the two JOBS situation to the time I went to the Fortune 100 corporate company.

There has to be a Better, Proven, Way!

Enter multi-level marketing. Why is it that people don't take multi-level marketing seriously as a real alternative profession?

I'll tell you why. Because they just don't get it, and they don't get it because the sponsors out there recruiting are weak. Even eighty percent of the people in multi-level marketing don't get it! Sure those eighty percent make a decent lifestyle enhancement and because of the nature of the beast they continue to hold onto their lifestyle enhancements. Good for them—they have learned an important philosophy or core principle—"don't quit."

What are the Alternatives?

Let's take a gander. Traditional marketing business models like retail, direct mail and direct sales marketing are the safe bets for an aspiring entrepreneur at first glance, but they offer little benefit to the entrepreneur. After the overhead is evaluated and all risk is said and done, fifteen percent profit at best is what you can hope for. FIFTEEN PERCENT!!! That is what you can expect after two or three years, not off the bat. You put up with all the hardships: hiring, firing, leases, overhead, your life energy, and savings or credit. Maybe you get a system that has proven success like a Mickey D's, but who has One Million Bucks to spend and a franchise that is on its way out? Not to mention all you did was buy the name for the million! You still have to go to Burger University and pay them an additional One Hundred Thousand for learning the ins and outs of the franchise. Now you have a SYSTEM in place and with another, I don't know million or so, you will have a nice location and are ready to get a return of (2.5 million x .15 = 375,000). $375,000.00 MAYBE in two or three years. Divide that by the three years and you have $125,000.00. Might as well stay in your middle class job.

Multi-Level Marketing: What It Is

Multi-level marketing is best understood by realizing the benefits of sharing experiences via word of mouth. Do you know of anyone that ever received a return for telling someone about a great restaurant, store, service or club? In multi-level marketing that is exactly what goes down. You tell a friend, they like what you told them, and they pass it forward. For doing that, you get a check. And they will too! It's that simple.

Don Failla has an amazing presentation. He calls it the *45 Second Presentation* and I use it all the time, as do my team members. You and your prospects may have opinions about multi-level marketing. In fact, most people do. The only way you can succeed in this industry is to address these issues upfront and in a jiffy! More about this later.

Multi-Level Marketing: What It Is NOT

I was 23-years-old or something like that when I met this smooth guy. Osman was his name. I'll never forget the dude because he was really charismatic, drove a nice car, spoke like he was in a commercial for Chrysler telling me about the Corinthian leather and about to invite me to some far off Paradise Island with someone in the back yelling "the plane, the plane, boss, the plane!" I know I may be dating myself, but that reference was to Ricardo Montalban the coolest cat I ever grew up watching on TV (other than Elvis Presley that is). But, I digress. Osman was currently sharing the vision of this amazing organization called Carico. Now this company is still around today, which is a testament to this type of marketing and why choosing a company with American roots is imperative. See, when a company is the manufacturer of the products it promotes it has control over everything, and MANY great companies who have stood the test of time are American manufacturing companies. The point is that they had things that people love to have, China, Crystal, Cookware, etc. The stuff was of great quality and of a great high price. It was always going to be the same quality because they controlled the assembly line. This form of marketing, although very successful for some, didn't work for me. It is called Direct Sales Marketing. Other forms of direct marketing are, but not limited to: insurance sales, vacuum cleaners, the Avon person, Tupperware, even Real Estate and Travel. This is many times confused for multi-level marketing, but the difference is really that direct sales marketing is seller based and the earnings come when YOU make the sales. If you're not selling, you're not earning. Mostly the items are higher ticket items and are one-time sales items in some of these franchises, i.e., water filters, or time-shares. Also, as you build your team of sales distributors there is a profit share component on their sales too. I'm just not that guy that will go door-to-door, or cold call you, igniting fear and the dangers of your water and why you need ME to give YOU this upside down reverse inverse UV light, organic diaphragm based super-duper clean, save the world, filtration system, oh, and you can have it for an incredible discount! That's just not me.

I was, however, attracted to the idea of brick and mortar franchises. The more I dove into RETAIL marketing, the more I realized that I just didn't have what it took—which was LOTS of money to get started. I did however exhaust every venue trying to make that possibility come true.

In-depth research led me to understand that there was a difference in being self-employed and an entrepreneur. I already knew that being an employee was not for me, even if I was the boss. Also, there was this little thing called ROI or return on investment. ALL traditional business goes through a start-up phase. The curve of this initial growth phase is usually fairly sharp in the beginning, and then the business stabilizes and begins experiencing a more normal growth rate as it matures. For an average business, this process takes about two to three years. Since starting any business is considered a relatively risky investment, I wasn't feeling good about the idea in the end.

Necessity is the Mother of Invention
…An idea is born…

In 2008 I was in the worst possible shape of my life at 5'11", 278 pounds, stressed to the bone working in a high profile global leader company specializing in infrastructure and business intelligence software. I traveled 80% of the time, and the 20% I was home I was even more stressed—worried that I'd wake up tomorrow and they would realize I wasn't being productive and profitable. Every time the phone would ring from California I would fear I'd be losing my job. I felt the upper management was forgetting me due to the out of sight, out of mind concept. I wasn't a happy camper to say the least. Those who truly suffered the brunt were my three kids for who I wasn't there for "physically." When I was, I wasn't pleasant to be around. I lived like that for ten years!

Exposure to the multi-level marketing sales model came accidentally. I saw a product that I needed, I bought it, and then months down the road I realized the organization had implemented multi-level marketing. Since I enjoyed my results I continued reordering the products and remained active, which meant I had the potential to make some money. All I had to do was share what I was doing. I started to use these products in my day-to-day routine and I became affectionate to the brand. I began to share my new health, fitness and belief with anyone who was struggling with similar health issues, which was really anyone I had been working with or simply in my circle of influence. It was really pretty easy. I simply used the product and became a product of the product. When someone came to me and asked me about my transformation, or something related to the product; I would go into share mode and honestly I may have scared away more people than I shared with.

It Hit Me that Multi-Level Marketing was a REAL Business

However, first some life lessons had to be learned...

I had an AH-HA moment—when I had a personal life-changing scare. But I have to explain a little about my past. It was 1989. I was fresh out of the Marine Corps and when I came home at the age of 20, I associated myself with less desirable friends. This association led to an arrest one evening and eventually my conviction for possession of illegal drugs. It was Miami in the Miami Vice era. I'm not trying to validate my behavior, glamourize it or rationalize it, I simply am explaining the time, the place, and the mindset. Quickly, the realization of the war on drugs hit me and I took one hundred percent of the responsibility. I'm a firm believer in that we all have choices to make and that these choices are ours to own. It was no one's fault but my own for not being the man my mother had brought up. My honesty and remorsefulness was the salvation of this situation. I was given more than a slap on the hand, but I didn't have to go to prison! I have this blemish on my record because I pleaded guilty to these charges and in return for my honesty, service to the country, my clean record to that point and that I was simply an idiot; the prosecution was very lenient, and conviction for the charges were on paper. This is important now because 20 years later, due to immigration law changes and after the September 11th tragedy, while coming into the US from a business trip to Mexico, Immigration and Custom Enforcement (or I.C.E.) at the airport flagged me. It was just a usual workday for me as a Global Software Architect. This particular day I worked at a telecommunications customer in Mexico City, and when done I went to the airport and flew home, like I'd done thousands of times over the previous decade. This time (ironically this new software was implemented by MY Company and with MY help) for the U.S. Department of Defense (DOD), the U.S. Department of Homeland Security (HLS), the U.S. Immigration and Custom Enforcement (ICE) and the U.S. Department of Justice (DOJ). The software flagged me and the agent asked me if I had ever had an altercation in the legal system in the past. I thought back, replied yes, and told him that it was 20 years ago, 1989.

His body language let me know this would not be a happy day. He said to another officer, "I can't believe this just happened, I gotta get out of here. My kid's got a birthday party…." Blah, blah, blah. I was starting to get nervous. Then he said, "It seems you pleaded guilty to a charge that was never looked at by an immigration judge, and that's the problem." I was mind boggled. What does that mean? I was taken into the back room, and after 12 hours of examination still not told anything. Eventually they explained that because I wasn't naturalized as a citizen and rather a permanent resident, and because I had a conviction for a drug offense, that I was now eligible for deportation from this country. Bear with me. I'm getting to why MLM is a great business model. So, now I am going through what was called the process of removal from the United States, i.e., Déportation Proceedings! Me, a United States Marine Corps (USMC) veteran, being detained for stupidity 20 years earlier at the age of 19 turning 20! I was floored. I had been an outstanding legal citizen paying taxes since I was 13, contributing to our country in the 28% bracket at that time, and like that, I was being put through this process. Long story short, I was detained by Immigration and Customs Enforcement (ICE), and DETAINED (that's the politically correct term used by them to deter the fact that they just incarcerated a perfectly innocent and contributing citizen). This detainment, incarcerated in an immigration prison, which stretched for almost one year, caused my wife who was currently in medical school, and just had a baby, to have to juggle everything. Can you even begin to imagine? I lost my JOB with a company that I'd given 10 years to with not even a blink of an eye. No loyalty, no empathy. I lost my house to foreclosure in the worst possible era of mortgages in this country. I had cars repossessed. I felt totally helpless from my situation.

In the end I was released. There was a substantial hit financially to my family and closest friends who poured over eighty thousand dollars into my situation. I was caught up in a legal mess that actually took me away from my life, family and hard worked freedoms. Just like that it was all gone—and I was gone, detained in an immigration prison, for almost a year! I was out of my comfortable, safe, and sure suburban life, and my wife and kids were left with all our debt, and bills, and stresses that I had previously juggled and dealt with as the main source of income. It was like I was DEAD, but still able to see it all going down!

I returned home almost a year later, embarrassingly to my parents' home (who I'm eternally grateful to for taking in my wife and two infant daughters). It was evident to me what a very challenging time for them it had been as well. As I came home my wife, who was then in her last year of medical school, said to me: "If it wasn't for the five hundred dollars that Beach Body sent you every month I would have had to drop out of medical school!" It was then, at that very moment, that I realized that the life I had, and you have right now, is an illusion!

Any one of a thousand things can happen to you and all you have worked for could be gone in a flash! It was in that moment that I realized the value of what is called residual income.

It's All About the Residual, Baby

I began to educate myself and learn all I could about how to create more and more of it.

Once you realize the value of residual income you quickly adopt an approach to create more. But it isn't until you reach the precipice that you appreciate it. With this book you create a map for seeking truths, for opening your mind, a Socratic method if you will. Take the definition of this philosophical approach as defined by Gregory Vlastos, a Socrates scholar and professor of philosophy at Princeton who writes: the method makes philosophical inquiry "a common human enterprise, open to every man." Instead of requiring allegiance to a specific philosophical viewpoint or analytic technique or specialized vocabulary, the Socratic method "calls for common sense and common speech." And this, he says, "is as it should be, for how man should live is every man's business."

To me it makes perfect sense. I will apply an exhaustive effort asking questions on the subject of residual income as it is based on a common human enterprise, networking, and it is open to anyone willing to put in the part-time effort to create full-time wealth. So should you! I also like the idea of not being tied to a specific viewpoint, or allegiance to a product, or even having to have a silver tongue. All you need is some common sense, which most of us have. You know you are really onto something great, because just about then is when you can't help but share it.

Here is an example of how much money you need to invest at different interest rates to generate the same residual income that you can earn from this type of business approach.

$200 Per Month		$600 Per Month		$800 Per Month		$1,000 Per Month	
Interest Rate	Amount in Bank	Interest Rate	Amount in Bank	Interest Rate	Amount in Bank	Interest Rate	Amount in Bank
2%	$120,000	2%	$362,000	2%	$480,000	2%	$600,000
3	80,000	3	240,000	3	320,000	3	400,000
4	60,000	4	180,000	4	240,000	4	300,000
5	48,000	5	144,000	5	192,000	5	240,000
6	40,000	6	120,000	6	160,000	6	200,000
7	34,286	7	102,857	7	137,143	7	171,429
8	30,000	8	90,000	8	120,000	8	150,000
9	26,667	9	80,001	9	106,667	9	133,334
10	24,000	10	72,000	10	96,000	10	120,000

$2,000 Per Month		$4,000 Per Month		$5,000 Per Month		$10,000 Per Month	
Interest Rate	Amount in Bank	Interest Rate	Amount in Bank	Interest Rate	Amount in Bank	Interest Rate	Amount in Bank
2%	$1,200,000	2%	$2,400,000	2%	$3,000,000	2%	$6,000,000
3	800,000	3	1,600,000	3	2,000,000	3	4,000,000
4	600,000	4	1,200,000	4	1,500,000	4	3,000,000
5	480,000	5	960,000	5	1,200,000	5	2,400,000
6	400,000	6	800,000	6	1,000,000	6	2,000,000
7	342,857	7	685,714	7	857,143	7	1,714,285
8	300,000	8	600,000	8	750,000	8	1,500,000
9	266,667	9	533,334	9	666,668	9	1,333,335
10	240,000	10	480,000	10	600,000	10	1,200,000

Chapter 2: Not Just for Friends and Family Anymore

My first exposure to anything like multi-level marketing was in the 1980's. Since then I have been tempted by countless acquaintances, true friends, and even family to join the most amazing thing EVER! Let me see, there was the water filtration, and cool china company, there was the shake company of the 1980's, the perfume and jewelry one, then there was that calling card one too, then there were so many others that I just was sick and tired of being sick and tired of hearing about this type of business. I became weary of the old friend that found my number magically, even though I had changed my phone number three times in 30 years.

It made me weary of old friends wanting to rekindle our relationship and I just avoided everyone—until the Facebook era that is.

So this is what I am saying: Do yourself a favor. Stay away from your friends and family! Yes, I said it, and so does one of the oldest books in existence today! The Bible reads in at least three places including the books of Luke, Mark and Matthew that "no prophet is accepted in his own hometown." Now what does that mean? Doesn't every single multi-level marketing business model you see teach you that you should make a list of family and friends and go to selling/sharing? They may hide the list under creative names like fast and furious five, longtime bros lists, or my favorite network book. (I do think this is a great idea if you use the network book for new prospects so you can follow-up with them, keep the dates you last contacted them, their phone numbers and their friends names too. But most importantly, create real lasting relationships).

You are the King/Queen of Your Castle, but Avoid Selling There

"It takes 20 years to build a reputation and five minutes to ruin it."—Warren Buffett

Remember this? "Friends don't let friends drive drunk." I tell you, real friends don't reach out to old friends luring them to a drink, lunch, or another event on the pretense of getting to know them and rekindling a friendship—when the true intention is to corner them with your unique opportunity! No, that is dead wrong and I'll be honest with you right here and now. They don't care about your transformation or your revolutionary gizmo. They don't want to be a part of your movement to save the world or how to be a part of those that save humanity. All they want was what you reached out to them for; all they are looking for is you. You said, "it's been a while—let's fix this distance thing" and if they say yes, all they are expecting is for you to be a friend.

Misleading someone is simply not honorable and no matter how you slice your intention, your ultimate goal was to pitch your product, and your presentation. That is not putting good things into the universe.

Tracy Biller, Author of eBooks, Audio and Reports like The Winner's Edge, says: It's easy to succeed in MLM when you recruit the right people, and the official guide to MLM success validates this by writing "the primary reason why people fail in MLM is because they are recruiting the wrong people." Which is exactly why I failed the first five years.

For nearly five years I did exactly what my up-line "heavy hitters" told me to do. Plus, during those five years I brought every MLM book and tape I could find and I applied everything I learned from the "experts." You name it and I did it.

The results for those five years was that I didn't even come close to achieving my goals.

How, Then, Do You Proceed? Comfortable Being Uncomfortable

IF it makes you squirm a little, then you are growing. The people who have succeeded in this business didn't do it by selling to their friends and family. They did it by finding people outside their comfort zone, and frankly that does mean "cold or lukewarm leads." But, don't be scared, because your mentor will be with you hand-in-hand through the process, so it won't feel like being out in the cold.

The Socrates Level Marketing™ Philosophy

Socrates Level Marketing™ is teaching people to be teachers, asking questions and finding natural answers, which can be passed on down generations. SLM™ puts the effort on sponsorship. Sponsorship is when you take a fresh new person in your organization and grow them into an exact duplicate of you. Why is this important? Because most multi-level marketers recruit. A recruit is brought in and left to fend for himself or herself. This causes confusion and frustration and propagates the stigma associated with our industry. People who are left to fend for themselves are going to naturally go to people they already know to sell a product because to not do so is uncomfortable. Instead of giving your prospect just the company material and then haphazardly walking them through their company website, you give them a curriculum just like any institution of learning would. I actually would lend them what they need and tell them you will be back to get it in a short time frame. This creates urgency. The curriculum contains books, authors, and personal development tools to learn what it means to actually be in marketing, specifically MLM. What you just did was indicate that this venture is one that is going to take some effort, albeit a part-time effort, and that it is an effort that has vastly larger return on investment than any other traditional method of employment or investment, short of coming across another Google Company IPO opportunity. It gives the prospect time and space to explore the idea of MLM and ask questions before they jump into the pan and burn themselves. And if they Invest, Learn, and Teach (I.L.T.) as my mentor Ray Higdon coined, they will attain a level of professionalism, develop a philosophy that will carry and propel them into a change of mindset. As I previously mentioned, one of the best materials I have read for training is <u>Don Faillia's *45 Second Presentation*</u>. It is an easy read and goes through the exact process of *honest intention* and creating a flowering and enduring business in MLM.

While doing this you have your team members realize that a real networking list/book is about acquaintances. The reality is that your future business partners and superstars that will help you create a part-time fortune will **NOT** come from your close list of friends and family. No, that wasn't déjà vu. I am repeating myself. My personal research has shown that most "superstar network marketers" that will create a nice residual income for you are simply one or two degrees of separation.

> *"It may seem odd but if you think of relationships in other areas of your life, this is more or less the norm. If you are married or are in a relationship, chances are, your spouse was NOT a childhood friend that you grew up with. It is most likely someone that you met from someone else or someone you met randomly. But it is NOT someone you had known for years growing up."*—Simon Chan

The same applies to your multi-level marketing business.

Or, they will come from a referral of someone else you know but NEVER someone you know directly well.

What Influential People Say About Network Marketing

"[Network Marketing is] a tremendous contribution to the overall prosperity of the economy."
—Tony Blair, Former British Prime Minister

"...you don't need to create a business plan or create a product. You only need to find a reputable company, one that you trust, that offers a product or service you believe in and can get passionate about."
—David Bach, Author of the New York Times best-seller, *The Automatic Millionaire*

"...the first truly revolutionary shift in marketing since the advent of 'modern' marketing at P&G and the Harvard Business School 50 to 75 years ago."
—Tom Peters, Legendary Management Expert and Author of *In Search of Excellence* and *The Circle of Innovation*

"...a home-based business offers enormous benefits, including elimination of travel, time savings, expense reduction, freedom of schedule, and the opportunity to make your family your priority as you set your goals."
—Zig Ziglar, Legendary Author and Motivational Speaker

"...How the best organizations of the future might run—in the spirit of partnership and freedom, not ownership and control."
—Jim Collins, Author of *Built to Last* and *Good to Great*

"What works is delivering a personal, relevant message to people who care about something remarkable. Direct Sellers are in the best position to do this."
—Seth Godin, Best-selling Author of *Permission Marketing, Unleashing the Ideavirus* and *Purple Cow*

"Direct Selling is actually one of the oldest, most respected business models in the world and has stood the test of time."
—Donald Trump, Billionaire Businessman and Owner of the Trump Network

"The Direct Selling business model is one that can level the playing field and close the gap between the haves and have-nots."
—Ray Chambers, Entrepreneur, Philanthropist Humanitarian and Owner of Princess House

"…best-kept secret of the business world."
—Roger Barnett, New York Investment Banker and Owner of Shaklee

"The best investment I ever made."
—Warren Buffet, Billionaire Investor and Owns three Direct Selling/Network Marketing companies

"From 2006 to 2016, there will be ten million new millionaires in the U.S. alone…many emerging from Direct Selling."
—Paul Zane Pilzer, World-Renowned Economist and Best Selling Author of *The Next Millionaires*

"…Direct Selling gives people the opportunity, with very low risk and very low financial commitment to build their own income-generating asset and acquire great wealth."
—Robert T. Kiyosaki, Author of *Rich Dad Poor Dad* and *The Business of the 21st Century*

"Network Marketing has come of age. It's undeniable that it has become a way to entrepreneurship and independence for millions of people."
—Stephen Covey, Author of *The Seven Habits of Highly Effective People*

"You strengthen our country and our economy not just by striving for your own success but by offering opportunity to others…"
—Bill Clinton, Former U.S. President

Chapter 3: Viable Business Marketing Strategy

In regards to starting a business, multi-level marketing is lower cost, lower overhead and lower risk than any other way I've found to start a business. It has many leverage points within the strategy. Customer support and relations, distributions and logistics issues are not your problem anymore. Research and development information is already provided about your products. Many times the competition and training resources are all on someone else's dime without you going through the pain of hiring and funding all those positions and learning all those processes. Sounds very much like a FRANCHISE, right? That's right! You are buying into a system and if you do and follow the system you WILL have successes in your future.

No matter what MLM company you are with, what product you have or what team is there to support you when you start, you are a new company in and of yourself. This is your business and you are a new breed of entrepreneur. YOU are the CEO despite how long the company has been around. In multi-level marketing the same wind blows on all of us. If that scares you, let me reassure you by telling you one more thing, even though you are in business for yourself you are definitely NOT in business by yourself. Just like the multitude of franchise opportunities available for the right price, you are also buying into a franchise ideology. Only with this one, you can get into it for as little as $25.00 in some cases and as much as a few thousand dollars based on your motivation level and commitment. Does it make a difference? Yes, right? Absolutely...NOT. What makes a difference is YOU. Do you recognize the opportunity and have the desire, hunger, motivation, and a coachable mindset? Because I repeat the same wind blows on all of us, and how you harness it is how fast you go.

Philosophy, WWSD? What Would Socrates Do? The Socratic method in its simplest form would have you ask many questions creating a common sensual approach.

Do You Want to (Insert Your Idea Here)? Yes or No?

There was an event that a friend of mine and I were at recently. I will talk about the power of "showing up and going up" a little later. Right now I want to share that I was at this event and not unlike other events the movers and shakers get a chance to prance across the stage. A man from India walked up on stage. He was very well dressed with a very humble and soft mannered personality. He walked up to the microphone and said in a very heavy accent: "I have been in this country for six months now. I came here to be with my children who were graduating from school and getting really great science and technology jobs, when Bill talked to me about this company. I tried the product and shared it with everyone I met, and then I received a check. And I am very happy. I love America and I love that I buy two cars, one for me and one for my wife whom I just brought to America two weeks ago. I love America and I LOVE THIS COMPANY. WOOOOHOOO!"

He waved and walked off the stage. I could see the rage swelling up on my friend's face so I said to him, "Let's go Socratic!"

We went looking for him and when we met up with him, of course we introduced ourselves. As soon as the pleasantries were done, we asked him all kinds of questions. The main one was how he grew the company so quickly, not having known anyone and only sharing the products?

He smiled at us and said,

"I never shared the products any more after I received my first check."

We were puzzled, and then we asked, "How did you succeed?"

He said, "I ask (the person who is interested), do you want to make money—yes or no? If they say yes, I call my team members and have them explain (the product or the MLM system), if (they say) no, then I ask someone else." Meaning he doesn't bother trying to sell them anything at all.

My friend asked, "Well, what if they ask you "how" (how are you going to make money) before they say no?"

He smiled again and said "(Then I say) I will tell you, but first answer, do you want to make money, yes or no?"

As simple as that question may seem right now, be honest with yourself and ask that question of yourself, and everyone you determine is a prospect. Be sure you understand your target audience, i.e. your avatar, thoroughly. There are two things going on here. The first thing is that you have a product that is being moved. It could be a shake or it could be a vacation package or a service…whatever. The second thing is the business—the ability to grow your business partner organization!

In order to make his organization grow the fastest, this man discovered he no longer needed to sell people on the product at all. He only talked with people who were interested in running the business and making money. This is a pretty out there concept for most people.

Most people fall into the first category, initially users of the product. They may eventually be a long shot business partner, but you have no way of knowing that from the start. In fact, I wasn't interested initially in the business in my latest multi-level marketing involvement. It was an unexpected miracle and it will happen that way for many people you introduce as well. But, there will come a time when the prospect will slip and ask you the question about your involvement with your organization and that's when you must be very clear and ask, "Do you want to make money—yes or no?"

The 4 Steps and Core Principles of Socrates Level Marketing™
Interrupt, Engage, Educate and Offer (Close)

1) Interrupt the pattern: My 16-year-old Tyler is an amazing baseball player, not because he's my son, but because he is seriously amazing. He may be one of the best short stops in all of South Florida. I hate to admit it, but I am a football and hockey guy, having played linebacker and right wing myself, so baseball wasn't the sport that caught my enthusiasm. He explained to me the other day the importance of a good change up by the pitcher. The key is the batter never sees a difference in the ball's release as it leaves the pitcher's hands, but what he had become accustomed to, as a fastball is now a slower ball or a curveball or knuckleball. In a sport where a strong arm has become a

commodity, a changeup helps pitchers break the pattern of fastballs to get the ball past the plate.

In Socrates Level Marketing™ we want to master the art of interruption because it allows for focused attention on what we want to get across. Your company will undoubtedly have a system, a game plan. That's what you want to set into motion. My Indian story guy broke a pattern, and went right into the system. He got people on 3-way calls, invited them to watch a video, and maybe invited them to an event. I don't know what it is for you, but you now have the ball rolling where it wasn't a minute ago. Do you want to develop an infallible system? Then keep reading because right around the corner I'll give you another seven steps to developing a seven-figure prospecting approach. Now that you've interrupted the pattern, what's next?

2) Engage your prospect: This doesn't mean run out and buy them a wedding ring! It means make them feel like what you are sharing is safe. Make them feel warm and fuzzy. Many people who are successful in marketing use what is called a Unique Selling Proposition (USP). Billions are spent every year on this kind of marketing and I'm giving it to you right here and now! Remember, I promised a seven-step, seven-figure prospecting approach? It's all part of this engagement step.

A) Know your Avatar: i.e., WHO is your prospect? WHO do you want to move to a decision? WHO are you trying to persuade? WHO is your target audience? Everything starts with the WHO?

Knowing who you want to be your prospect.

"You can't hit a target you cannot see, and you can't hit a target you do not have."—Zig Ziglar

So right now you're like, okay Socrates, I get it brother, but that's not enough information. How do I do that? And that is why I included a questionnaire in this book on defining your AVATAR. Listen, if you want to BOOM! your business, you have to get clear. Clarity is KING in all things marketing.

- What keeps them awake at night?
- What do they fear the most?
- What trends are occurring in their business?
- What do they drive?
- What are they eating?
- What makes them happy?
- Who are they married to?
- How many kids do they have?
- How old are they?
- What are their needs?
- What do they fear?
- What is *their dream?*

The more specific, the clearer you can be with your Unique Selling Proposition, the more razor sharp your interruption and engagement can be. In fact, if you do this step your USP will become an ESP...no, not like in reading their minds, but close! It means "Extraordinary Sensational Offer," with a *powerful promise.*

Continuing with the engage step now you have directed your product and business to your prospect. They are interested—but only for a limited time. Statistically they will get bored of you in about 2 minutes and 7 seconds according to studies by the New York Times.

B) Get their Attention: You have done your homework. You know this person well and they are there with you engaged 100%. If you want to keep their interest, you better be UNIQUE and COMPELLING now. Why? Because if you aren't unique you are just another retail store, another gas station, but what if you're GEICO? Then you're so easy a ?????; if you're Domino's you can get your pizza in ???? or ????, and of course the answer is "that a caveman can do it" and "30 minutes or it's free!" Even if you are challenged in closing this prospect right now, it remains imprinted that there is no other choice but you.

C) The NINJA (Hidden Benefit): This is one of my favorite parts of engagement! Think about it. You can set yourself up, create your "Extraordinary Sensational Offer" with a *powerful promise* (ESP) and then slide in the hidden benefit about your "thing." (I'm talking about the business). How do you set that up? You slip in a strategic comment that appeals to the subconscious interest of your particular avatar, alluding to the business that will allow them to do more of what they like. Examples are, if you are in health and fitness, "Well you can choose to do it the old fashioned way or choose to do it in 10 days," "There's no selling involved, if someone asks you a question, there's an entire team ready to receive your calls," "Put fat burning on auto pilot, and go play golf with me," etc....

D) Get them to the "YES" path: There is nothing quite like getting people to physically nod their heads and verbally respond affirmatively. It's quite magical really. But you'll have to ask the right questions. Would it be OK if we took a few minutes to explain this? Would it be OK if you had the right tools to succeed at your own business? Would it be OK if you learned one thing you could use right now that would make a difference in EVERY part of your life today? Would it be OK if I told you what to say? Would…It…Be…OK?

E) DRAMA: I know! No one likes drama. This is a drama free zone. Leave the drama at the door, right? WRONG! The good news is that you are in show business! The bad news is that you are in show business! You need to practice your USP/ESP, your NINJA skills, your ability to do it all in under 2 minutes, 7 seconds and at some point agitate the situation, because people, as much as they say they hate it, love to side with an issue that they negatively resonate with.

"It's just sad how health care workers are just so entirely out of shape these days!" "They peddle chemicals and pills, and live a do as I say not as I do life," "I'm so glad that there is movement that aims to change all that!" Notice the <u>problem</u> was pitched, the <u>agitation</u> was made, and the <u>solution</u> provided!

"Is there anyone left we can trust?" "It's bad enough that drug firms made BILLIONS from pain pills linked to heart attacks. And now, these swindlers are trying to get their teeth in alternative medicine too," "At last, there is ME you can trust." Again the use of <u>Problem,</u> <u>Agitation</u> and <u>Solution.</u>

Now this is a live wire. Be careful. Use of it is highly effective, but make sure you deliver a solution after you agitate. Remember these three steps: <u>Problem</u>, <u>Agitate</u>, and <u>Solution</u>! If you miss any of these steps, don't expect birthday cards this year!

F) YOU: BOOM! Enter the YOU. You are the reason for the season, and it's what creates rapport with the prospect. You enter as the solution by humanizing yourself, by using stories that resonate with your avatar, shared experiences, shared hardships, and by revealing shared dreams. People join "the mission" because they are interested in the person, not the company. So why not give them the best impression of yourself? This is not an easy task, but with practice can become part of any conversation after an introduction. Five things to remember in your arsenal: Pets, kids, love/marriage, current events/gossip, and sports!

G) Brand yourself: if you learn anything here it's that no matter what you are sharing, it's YOU that is sharing it. YOU are in the business of decisions, not anything else. Your job description is to make the prospect make a decision to use your product, become a business partner or both. You are not a health distributor, life coach, or independent whatever. You are you and you happen to have experienced an amazing opportunity and you need to share it. Period. Would a friend not share an opportunity to another if they really believed in it? That's the last of the engage section.

3) Educate: It is now time to educate the prospect. They must see the logic in using your product, joining your team or both. Create relevance by framing what you are offering as a solution, following the "what's in it for me" (WIIFM) approach. Provide enough detailed, quantifiable and specific information to allow consumers to logically understand how and why your product or service solves their problem—but don't stop there. You may have given them enough information to Google your product, and then instead of making a purchase from you they make one from your competitor! Prove that you offer the best value available by defining key issues, presenting a convincing argument and sharing credible evidence that you are the only possible source to meet your prospect's needs. This is where social proof is helpful. There is nothing like a real life testimony to relieve anxiety, build trust and create authority, so share those at this time.

4) Close: Compel the consumer to take action through an offer. Present a low-risk way to take the next step: "Oh by the way, it's totally 100% guaranteed, no questions asked."

"Today you can get $50.00 off with this gift card."

Etcetera.

Chapter 4: Expertise Creation

There are definite stigmas you must get over when you choose to become a professional in multi-level marketing, but before I address this realize the following:

The global sales force of network marketers and direct sellers reached an all-time high in 2014 with nearly 100 million* people involved! This number is up 3.4% up since 2013.

This is a vibrant and diverse group:
- Some are entrepreneurs—small business owners building their own businesses.
- Some do direct selling part-time to earn extra income for their families.
- Everyone involved gains new skills, new friendships, and greater self-esteem.
- Most contribute to the charitable organizations their companies are involved in.
- Many were customers of the products before they became representatives.
- Some choose to enjoy the discounted products and decide not to sell, at all.

- Retail sales hit record highs of US $182.8 billion* in 2014. The steady growth curve continues with an annual growth rate of 6.5% for the period from 2011-2014.

Top 10 Markets*:	Global Sales
#1 USA	19%
#2 China	17%
#3 Japan	9%
#4 Korea	9%
#5 Brazil	7%
#6 Germany	5%
#7 Mexico	4%
#8 France	3%
#9 Malaysia	3%
#10 UK	2%
	Regional Sales*:
Asia/Pacific	45%
North America	19%
South/Central America	18%
Europe	17%
Africa/Middle East	1%

*The World Federation of Direct Selling Associations figures for 2014 (www.wfdsa.org)

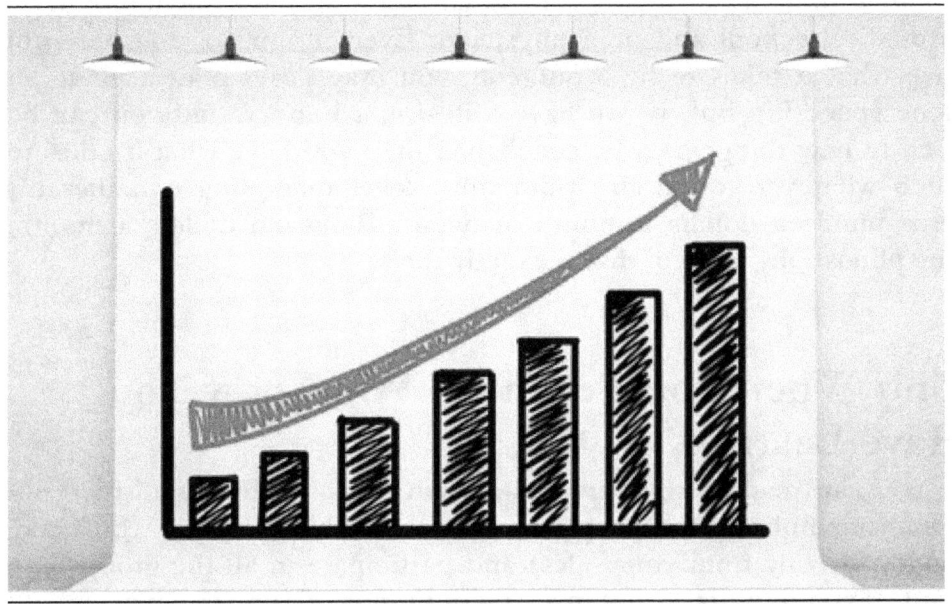

Source:

http://directsellingnews.com/index.php/view/smart_leadership_spurs_growth_at_rodanfields#.Vcvv7GCd5UQ

Get quick scheme—I don't think so! Don't just walk away from a company that promises huge profits or from that person that loves to show you their check—RUN!!!! Run as fast as you can in the opposite direction.

That's not ethical and I've yet to see any office based white collar colleague pull out their check and say "Ehhh? Ehhhhh? Not bad, right?"

It's just not what normal people do, and you know what? It shouldn't be done in multi-level marketing either. If you're lazy, a procrastinator, or have a hard time making decisions, or…and this one is a subconscious doozy, are scared of success, then this industry really may not be for you. There is no shame in that! You also may not be qualified to be a Certified Public Accountant, or have the ability to go to medical school and be a physician. Even if you do, you may not have what it takes to be a Surgeon, you may never pilot a plane let alone spaceship but, if you have a desire, a hunger, and you can be open to new things, i.e., be coachable, then you have what it takes to reach whatever you desire from multi-level marketing, whether it's three hundred dollars a month or twenty thousand dollars a month. The philosophy to all of that is exactly the same.

Only When You Teach Do You Know You Have Learned

You can read all the personal growth books, listen to all the cues from your upline, (the people above you in the company who make money directly from your sales) and participate in all the groups you want. If you don't take that investment in money, time or whatever and really digest it, and learn it by making it your own, then it's been a total waste of effort. You must teach what you have learned and do it while you are putting it all into action. This is the only way to know that you really know it yourself. I love the saying "teach and teach until you can hit the beach!"

Let me give you an example of common sense. Assume you just bought your dream car or boat! I'm talking a Lamborghini or a Hetaeras Yacht. Your best friend comes over and asks you for the keys to take it for a spin. Do you 1) throw them the keys or 2) ask them a series of questions, such as: Have you ever driven a high performance car with this type of clutch, or do you know how the helm works on the yacht? If the answer is throw them the keys, then congratulations! You are like 80% of the people in MLM today. Eric Worre calls these people the "Posers and Amateurs." Where the posers treat this as a meal ticket and think all they have to do is get lucky enough to share with a few hard workers, that they can skate along to riches, and the amateurs sort of take it a little more seriously, but can't put the pieces together.

It wasn't until I realized that I just don't know what I don't know—how can I? How can I know what I don't know if I don't know it yet? Consequentially, many of my upline knew as little as I did or less. But the moment I woke up and asked the right question, what is it that I don't know yet, things changed. What is it that Grant Cardone, Don Failla, Jim Rohn, Tom Big Al Schreiter, Eric Worre, Brandy Sinoto, Bob Proctor, Simon Chan, Terrence Gray, Bob Crisp, Sara Robbins, etc.—what is it they know that I NEED to know? What is it they DO, THINK, what kind of action do *they* perform daily, that I need to know? So I used the Socratic Method™ and applied the I.L.T. (Invest, Learn, Teach) model. That empowered me with tools that made me the authority in the room, because the fact is that as long as I knew more than anyone else in the room, people would gravitate toward me. The first thing that happened is I became a serious SLM™ entrepreneur. I graduated right then and there from amateur to professional.

Stop Hunting and Start Fishing

All of a sudden while I was putting in to action the knowledge I was gaining from all the big names in the industry, I realized that being that guy out there hunting—and waiting to pounce, many times irrevocably severing relationships—just wasn't a sustainable method…and it didn't duplicate. When I realized I needed to be the fisherman putting on the lure and waiting, that the fish would start coming to me. That is exactly what happened. Now I'm not saying that the fishing takes no preparation, not at all. You need to know what you are fishing for (avatar), you need to have the right bait (spoken and written copy material), and you have to be diligent (targeting via a campaign) and have patience and commitment, determination, and dedication (NEVER QUIT).

I grew up. I had matured. People were noticing too. People, who are always watching, whether I thought so or not, began to want to be around me, and ask me about what I did. When I owned the title of multi-level marketer, I began to respect my industry and it began to pay me. See, how could I ever have expected it to pay me if I never owned it? I became honest. When people asked me what I did for a living, I no longer said "scientist" or "software architect" or "life coach." I said I was in multi-level marketing. I never sold one single thing, and I simply explained what I did and how I lived with integrity. Sure, I knew who my avatar was all the time, so I spoke and shared based on which avatar was listening. That isn't dishonorable. If anything, it's the most honorable thing you can do—and my studies have indicated this is the best way.

There is a new world out there; all you have to do is open your eyes and ears. I know and have first hand knowledge that the 40/40/40 world is gone and getting even worse as you read this book. Going to work for 40 or more hours, for 40 or more years, and hope that you'll get 40% of your income back for retirement is insane. There is a boogeyman out there, lurking in the nebulous of "What am I going to do?" It isn't multi-level marketing though, it's without a doubt the illusion that owing ungodly amounts of money for school loans, business startup loans, leasing a lifestyle, and keeping up with "The Jones" is the real life monster. That paradigm is a flat out lie. The amazing thing is you can enter this industry part-time, and augment the 40/40/40 until you can eliminate it entirely. You can enjoy the fruits of the seeds you sowed and the countless other people you have helped along the way.

Chapter 5: Not About Product, but Relationships

"Happy are those who dream dreams and are ready to pay the price to make them come true."— Leon J. Suenens

It doesn't matter how good your product is or how awesome your support team is, the most important thing to do is build on relationships over time. You know Rome wasn't built in a day. There should never be a reason why you take a rejection from a prospect, EVER, in a personal manner. Someone not wanting your product is not a reflection on you. They simply just may not need it right *there* and *then*. No doesn't mean no forever, it just means no right now. Over time, by establishing and strengthening relationships you empower people to want to be around you. When people gravitate to you it validates your authority. It is a business built on people by people that care, and when you build that trust, when it is their time, they will find you.

By focusing on building the relationship, it will make you ultimately feel good, whether or not you sell a product to that person or they become part of the company. Forbes Magazine had this to say about it in an interview with Daria M. Brezinski Ph.D., a practicing psychologist and former marketing director for a multi-level marketing magazine that echoes these sentiments. "Many people don't realize that multi-level marketing companies are successful because they help people satisfy a number of important human needs, including feeling significant, having connections, learning something new, and making a difference. I have heard people in network marketing say again and again, 'I'm doing this because I'm meeting amazing people…making so many connections…and I feel so good about myself.'"

Dr. Brezinski's point is well taken and easy to see practiced by multi-level marketers. Many MLM and NM companies tout a three-to-five year plan to attain freedom and wealth, yet many of the people running company meetings have been in the business for five or ten years and still haven't left their full-time job or landed on easy street. "As it turns out," Dr. Brezinski notes, "when other human needs are being met, the members and consultants don't focus solely on the financial aspects."

What I hope you get out of this chapter is that you will get out of SLM™ what you put into it, but regardless you will have to be social, engaging and willing to speak to people. We call that prospecting, and without it there is simply just no way I believe you will succeed. Having said that, there is only a hand full of objections that people may have to wanting to be involved with you. If you "vibrate" at the same level as they do then you will handle all those objections out right, immediately. This is my way of saying you are listening with the purpose of understanding and not with the purpose of responding. Even then, there may be some who don't want to be involved no matter what; which is self-imposed, tough to catch, and hidden in many statements. It's the objection they have about themselves, the "I can't do this" limitation.

Chapter 6: Takeaway—BOOM!

"Wealth and power results from knowing things no one else knows."—Aristotle Onassis

I hope that in this book you acquired some peace in knowing that you are NOT alone. That every professional, every success story about a super star, started out as an amateur. I myself was in dire straits when multi-level marketing helped me realize there most definitely was a better way. I still have my degrees and I still enjoy chatting up a storm on current scientific developments, and information technology still gets me excited mentally and giddy, but, my profession is a Multi-Level Marketer and by using Socrates Level Marketing™ philosophies I can assure myself, and you, that there is never a shortage of prospects. They are everywhere!

The key to success is to expose your business to as many people as possible. The more people that know about your business, the better.

The paradigm shift I hope you adopt from this book is that your focus should be on five core principles—proven activities that help make money—and more importantly, can duplicate down to your team and help THEM make money. This will increase your residual stream and provide you with the ability to dream bigger than you have ever dreamed before.

Every day you (and your team) want to do the following:
- Add new people to your/their contact list
- Show the plan to new prospects
- Follow-up with old prospects
- Invest time in self development
- Communicate with your/their team

Core One: Contact Lists

The real purpose of a contact list is to announce to the world a launch of YOUR BUSINESS. That's right, you are "Officially Open For Business!" Do not make a contact list and end up in the NFL—no not the National Football League—but the "No Friends Left" scenario. Make this list as intensive as possible. You want to make it a huge deal. Release the news that you are now in business for yourself and you are excited about this professional and this extremely lucrative opportunity. TREAT SLM™ AS A TRADITIONAL BUSINESS and it will pay you better than a traditional business because you don't have the risks it has. Treat your multi-level marketing business like a million dollar business. When you think of yourself as having a traditional business instead of "just" a multi-level marketing business, your actions become more thought out and in line with common sense. By letting everyone know about your business in the REAL sense of the word, you have just eliminated your biggest threat—FEAR!

Core Two: Show the Plan to New Prospects

No matter what company you signed up with, they undoubtedly have a system in place. It's their GAME plan. You can't follow it if you don't understand it. If your upline isn't using it, then you need to be proactive and keeping with the "this is YOUR business" philosophy, find someone in the company who is using it and ask them to mentor you for at least 30 days. In that time you will have established a habit and seated a duplicable process you will never fail to share down. When you couple SLM™ core principles and your game plan you and your team will be unstoppable. This is the most valuable item I am sharing with you. Use your company leaders to mentor you, keep asking them until you find one you jive with and ask them for 30 days of accountability.

Get your product into the eyes, ears, and hands of all of your prospects. Remember nothing takes place of the energy and the momentum of bringing your prospects to a LIVE event, not Google hangouts, not FaceTime, not Skype. Real live interactions give you real live results.

Core Three: Follow-up with Old and New Prospects

If you simply don't follow up with leads or prospects you are probably missing out on 80% of the people you could be sponsoring. MOST people are NOT going to join in the very first conversation, so be sure to work smart sales follow-up into your SLM™ prospecting habits. The money is in the follow-up. With all my degrees and all my smarts, I took this for granted for way too long. Once I decided to become a professional multi-level marketer, the first thing I did was brand this five-core principle into my actual DNA, especially the follow-up.

Scenario One: "The No Show"

You invited them and they didn't show. Is that unusual? ABSOLUTELY NOT. In fact, it's darn right the norm. If you go with your emotions and take this personally, the usual reaction is a retort of enormous guilt laying and amateurish communication. Making them feel bad is just a sure way they will NEVER come and possibly may cost you friendship points and definitely trust. So what do you do? YOU APOLOGIZE! That is right. You take that opportunity to demonstrate your authority and what they missed out on. For example, "Hey ___, listen I wanted to apologize for not doing a better job of explaining what was happening last night. Last night we had a bunch of people show up. It was an amazingly cool thing. Listen I hope it's OK, I have to prioritize my time with those that DID show up, so I can reach out to you in the next couple of weeks or something. Hey, I have another call coming in. I have to run."…Why does this work? Because people want to be a part of the cool thing, the BIG thing, and they realize that you are actually not a joke, and will respect your time and invitation better next time. Remember: no does not mean no forever, just no right now.

Scenario Two: "Build Too Fast"

Another scenario is when I was involved with a company and when I began using the product I was so passionate about it, that I went crazy on the sharing and just enrolling record numbers of people. I didn't use any method or reason. I just beat people over the head with my charisma and the overwhelming idea that they HAD to get what I had. In failing to follow the Socrates Level Marketing™ philosophy, I failed to teach them in turn how to share it in an easy and duplicable way. In fact I had prospected so hard and so quickly it was inhumanly possible for me to even manage, let alone be a leader to that many people. So what did I do? What can you do? YOU APOLOGIZE! That's right, take ownership and be that guy or gal that people love to see accept that they messed up. The country forgave Former President Bill Clinton, Mel Gibson, and even Kanye West right? So, apologize, i.e. "Hey ____, listen, I really need to apologize to you. Well, see back when I shared ____ with you, I was just so passionate and simply just wanted to honestly affect as many people I could. Because I did it like that and I had NO idea of how to do this business I feel I failed you and let you down. I'm still with the company, just a lot more focused. Again, I just wanted to apologize and hope we can hang out and chill in the future in some way." That was the exact line I used on 489 people in 2014. Now, there was no pitch there and it should be that way. You are trying to regain your integrity and your posture of power in their minds and you know what, you did just that. On your next chat, and that should happen in the not too distant future, but with some cushion. Maybe seven days, "Hey ___, Socrates here. I was going through my online office and realized that you might actually be interested in some of our new products. Or might not be opposed to sharing some of your friends who would benefit from these things. In fact, and I know this may not be a fit for you, I'm curious if you know someone who would be OK with taking some extra vacations this year, or in need of paying off some debt?" This works because they want to be that guy or gal who takes the vacation and we all have debt that we want off our plates. But of course the point is to ask open-ended questions and find out what is important to them.

Scenario Three: "It's All About the Leads…Or Is It?"

Lastly it's all about the leads, the leads, the leads. No, seriously, it is all about the leads! But, what good is that stack of papers with a hundred names lying on the desk, or next to your bed, or on the dining room table? ZERO VALUE! So what do you do? NOPE! NO APOLOGIES! Here it's ACTION in a three-call format. You:

1. Call and REMIND them who you are and why you are calling them. Ask them to return your call.
2. 24 hours-ish. Very politely let them know you called yesterday, and that you are calling because they are on your list. And that "Hey if you are not open to making money from home let us know. We will remove you from the list."

3. 48 hours from the day two calls, call again and politely explain that you have called two times and that they will be removed from the list. They will NEVER be called again and that you wish them the very best life has to offer.

Why does that work? It is because on call three you have removed them off the list! People hate being off your list. That third call will get you lots of callbacks. It will, and it will definitely get you more than you not following up at all. Do you take them off your list for real? You move them to a different list, the list of people who didn't return the third call, for perhaps a more long-range follow up, if you need it or maybe you run into them again. Only the nasty and close-minded get 86'd in the Socrates Level Marketing™ philosophy. Why? Because no today is not no forever. Times change, people change, and your list is the Holy Grail.

Bonus Scripts: The SLM™ Way To Say Things

The focus should be on them, not you. Here is exactly what I say when I call my SLM™ leads:

"Hey there, this is Socrates, [I saw that you (inquired, bought, called me)] or [we spoke at (the coffee shop, office, bank, etc.)] and wanted to reach out to see how I can help you. Or I forgot to mention that I'm getting together with a group of other professionals and wanted to ask if it would be OK to invite you to check out this very lucrative opportunity. It may not be for you, but you'll have to take a look to decide. At the worse case, you may know someone that would be interested in the opportunity."

Then I listen and my goal is to get them to talk as much as possible. After listening I might ask those questions such as the ones I've included for you in the bonus chapter at the end of this book.

The goal, again, is to get them to talk, which will supply YOU with enough information to know which direction to move them toward. If I feel they may be a fit into the video presentation I direct them to that, if I feel they are an event person then I invite them to one of my many events, if I feel they are a knowledge based person then I get them on a 3-way call, all because I listened purposefully.

More About Leaving Voicemails

There is a lot of gold in leaving voicemails but most people do it totally wrong. The goal of a voicemail is to get a call back, not to explain your compensation plan or product. Leave a very simple voicemail. If you are NOT generating 30-50 leads per day, this is where you need to focus your energy to squeeze as much out of each lead as possible.

The First Voicemail

Leave a simple one saying, "Hey there, this is _____. I was referred to you, please give me a call back at xxxxx."

(You do NOT want to sound like a sales person or they probably will not call you back).

Another option you can play with is people are hooked on training like a chubby kid to cake. "Hey, this is ____, just calling to get your information to send you our free training. Call me back at _____ so we can get this out to you."

The Second Voicemail

This should give a slight bit more information such as, "Hey there, this is _____, yesterday you visited ____ on _____and I was just reaching out to see how I can help you. You can reach me at _____."

The Third Voicemail

This is where you do the takeaway. "Hey ___, this is ____. I just wanted you to know we are taking you off our list of people serious about _____. Wish you the best of luck and thanks for visiting us _____. There is more information at www.____.com. Take care and this will be the last time we call, good luck."

As I said earlier this is the money. You will get the most callbacks from this message as people respond well to the fear of loss.

Core Four: Invest Time in Self-Development

I can't tell you enough how this alone has changed my life over the last few years. I say all the time that SLM™ is a personal development course with a profit attached. I never say a paycheck because I could care less about a paycheck. It's continued profit I want, residual income, passive flow of everlasting cash. And the only way you will ever get this is by bettering yourself. YOU ARE the sum of the five people closest to you. There is no doubt about that. Attend as many courses in the industry, and supporting industries, as you can.

Core Five: Communicate with Your/Their Team

How can you sail your ship without constant adjustment of the sail? How can that crew reach their destination without a common goal? Ever see one of those sailing regatta world cups? A huge, humongous ship, and what looks like 50 or 60 people running around each other sharing and communicating with one goal in mind. They know what each mate is doing, they think alike, they talk alike, they move in unison and there are dozens of these ships out there! But only a few are in the lead. Is it the wind? Is it possible that the wind blows better for those few ships? NO!!! Not at all. The wind blows on them all equally, but it's the well-oiled team that steers the ship effortlessly in the best direction. The best paradigm is applied to the whole as one unit. It is the crew that trusts each other, communicates and has the common goal. In the end that one trophy belongs to all of them. You need to communicate with your team not just first generation but all the way down, tap rooting and sharing, because the truth is the super stars very rarely come on your first line. It happens, but it's the old adage of make a friend and meet their friends that makes you a super star in Socrates Level Marketing™ world.

Don't forget! You want to use the proven Socrates Level Marketing™ prospecting system in chapter 3. Be direct and Interrupt, Engage, Educate and Offer (Close).

Bonus

33 Network Marketing Answers!

Why Questions BOOM! Recruiting Versus Sponsoring

You have to ask questions before you get answers my friend. Let's address the elephant in the room first. You struggle with recruiting because you don't understand that what you need to do is sponsoring. You SPONSOR someone, then TEACH them how to do what you are doing—"building a BUSINESS OF THEIR OWN." RECRUITING is when you bring someone into the organization who is ALREADY experienced in network marketing and MLM. So if you struggle, it's because you think it is about selling someone a kit or package when the essence of multi-level marketing is about finding positive minded people that want more HEALTH, TIME, MONEY, etc....i.e., a better lifestyle. How do you find out if people want more? You ask them the right questions. Then you put them through your tools, i.e., Calls/Videos/Meetings/Events/etc.

How to Use These Scripts

You may want to print this and if you have a team, share it with them. Here is a word of advice. A good idea is having these questions close to your computer, your phone and within your reach when you are talking to prospects. Many of the mentors on www.SocTalks.com make this second nature, like breathing, like blinking. One well-placed question will free you from word vomit and get the prospect talking.

Here You Go! 33 Network Marketing Sponsoring Questions

1. I'm curious, would you be open to a side project that wouldn't interfere with what you are currently doing?
2. Hey, I'm just curious, would you be open to exploring another avenue of making a part-time income?
3. Would it be OK if I asked you what has recently changed in your life that has you open to a home business?
4. Ever wonder if there was a way to make money on Facebook?
5. Ever get the feeling you were meant to do something great?
6. I'm curious, if you had the money, would you jump at this opportunity?
7. I know you don't know, but if you did know, what would you really like to have in life?
8. I'm curious, how long will you have to continue working that many hours?
9. I just found out how I can travel more. Ever wish you could travel more?
10. Would it be okay if you could spend more time with your family?
11. I'm curious, would it be OK if someone were willing to show you how to make money from home, would you be open to that?

12. I'm curious, do you know that there are ways to create a decent income flowing into your bank account, whether you roll out of bed, or just roll over in bed?
13. I'm curious, what would your perfect job be?
14. I'm curious, what would your perfect life be like?
15. I'm confused, when you said you wanted to spend more time with your family, were you serious about that?
16. Everybody knows they should keep their options open. Do you keep your options open when it comes to making extra money?
17. I'm curious; do you know anyone that has been affected by the economy that might be open to making some extra money? Would it be okay if you introduced me so I can share the opportunity?
18. I'm curious, you know a few professionals like us. I am looking for a good financial planner/realtor/whatever to share a new lucrative opportunity that's just taking off in this area. I'm doing it part-time and from home, do you know any other professionals?
19. I'm curious; do you like helping other people? Would it be OK if you got paid to do so?
20. I'm curious; do you see yourself doing what you are doing 20 years from now?
21. Have you found what you are looking for? I'm curious. Will that provide ultimate freedom for you and your family?
22. If money were not an issue, what would you do for fun?
23. If money were not an issue, how would you help people?
24. I'm curious of what you see in a home business?
25. I'm curious, do you like what you are currently doing?
26. Everybody wants a change of sorts, what would you like to change about your current situation?
27. Would it be OK if I asked what challenges you have faced in the past?

28. I'm curious, what are your goals for this year? Would it be OK to ask "Why?"
29. Would it be OK to ask you what made you join a home business in the past? I'm curious, if you had the right teaching would you have had a better result?
30. I'm curious, what did you hope to get out of your last home business that you didn't get?
31. I'm curious, why do you have that impression? Where did you pick that up?
32. I'm curious, what was it you like MOST about the Video, the Call, the Meeting, the Webinar, etc.?
33. Would it be OK if I trained you in the exact way I was trained to create a part-time income stream?

Join the Conversation

Which of these Network Marketing Recruiting questions have you used? Which one was your favorite?

If you enjoyed this, and want more content like this, please comment and share at www.soctalks.com.

BOOM!

About the Author

I believe I will defer this chapter to my friends. But before I quote one of them I will tell you a little thing about Socrates Esteban Zayas. I am a lover of good Vodka and Dark Stout Beer. I love to really enjoy the things that make me feel free and alive, like Hang Gliding, Extreme Racing, i.e., Spartan Races and Ninja Warrior Obstacles, and Motorcycles. I will not compromise anything for the loss of time with my children. I pay my rent in the form of service, because that is the cost of taking up space on this planet. BOOM!

"I first met Socrates Zayas over the phone. His commanding voice 'booming' about the success he had with a 10-Day Transformation. His excitement and resolve was intoxicating. Well, as it turns out, that's just how he lives his life now. Peddle to the medal, full throttle, and his mission? His MISSION is to help as many people as he can to help themselves first, then to reach down and help others in turn. That is the legacy of Socrates Level Marketing™.

Socrates' passion for this industry is what gives multi-level marketing a "Good Name!" He has dedicated himself to teach anyone and everyone. He has no prejudice for any MLM/NM company on the planet. You'll see from those just looking to pay for their product/s all the way up to those who are ready to kick it up a notch and turn on the "BOOM! Factor!"

Why is MLM such a struggle for so many? Often it is core principles that are the missing link. DocSoc knows this. He's lived it. And he has seen it through his career in at least 10 MLM companies. He has created teaching tools that when coupled with actionable items become systems to follow at any stage. Everyone at every level of the network marketing business can raise the bar to "Socrates Level Marketing™!"

Unravel the myths around MLM and what the REAL opportunities are. Listen to the masterfully genuine interviews on www.SocTalks.com. Dispelling the false notions, yet more importantly instilling the vibrant magical lifestyles that can come from a love of helping others, the very root of this industry. And for the record, I'm not talking those bullshit lives of yachts and "caviar dreams," I'm talking real freedom, real connection with family and friends and living from a place of passion, abundance and love!

Speaking of bullshit. Let me just say one of the things I enjoy most about brainstorming with this bald genius. It is his "NO BS" approach to getting his message across AND ensuring that his message is understood. There's only one outcome when you put Socrates on your TEAM, and that outcome is success!

You may say what might "I" learn from this mystical creature called Socrates?

We grow and discover and learn through stories, stories on how things work, stories of how things were, and stories of how people did this, that, or the other thing. Here is a chance to peer into the life of a man who has overcome extreme obstacles, and who has failed many times in life only to succeed. In his words "he had no other choice!"

Put Socrates on your TEAM—and I'll see YOU at the TOP!"

Patricia Seixas, Naples, Florida

To contact Socrates:
Socrates Zayas, PhD
12401 W. Okeechobee Road, Unit 460
Hialeah Gardens, Florida 33018
305-775-4541
imdocsoc@gmail.com

www.ingramcontent.com/pod-product-compliance
Lightning Source LLC
Chambersburg PA
CBHW070933180526
45168CB00003B/1058